Language Readers

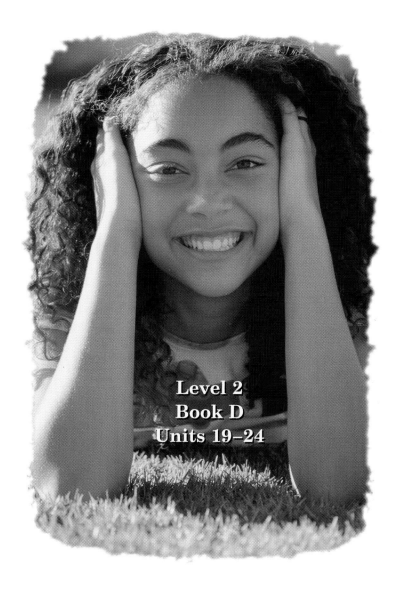

Level 2
Book D
Units 19–24

Jane Fell Greene
Judy Fell Woods

Text layout and design by Kimberly Harris
Cover design by Becky Malone
Cover Image © 2000 by Digital Vision Ltd.
Illustrated by Peggy Ranson

This product is in compliance with AB2519 California State
Adoption revision requirements.

Printed in the United States of America

Published and Distributed by

Sopris West
*Helping You Meet the Needs
of At-Risk Students*

4093 Specialty Place • Longmont, CO 80504 • (303) 651-2829
www.sopriswest.com

Contents

GRAM AND GRAMPS MARKS

UNIT 19

Phonology/Morphology Concepts

- If a syllable contains an **-r**, the /r/ phoneme controls the vowel phoneme.
  - There are three different **-r** controlled phonemes:
    1. /ar/ (car)
    2. /or/ (sort)
    3. /er/, /ir/, /ur/ (germ, sir, curt)
  - A syllable that ends with an **r-** controlled vowel is an **r-controlled syllable**.

Vocabulary

after	dirt	Herbert	porter	*come*
Art	escort	hornets	September	*some*
barn	far	Lester Sparks	short	*who*
bender	farm	market	spark	
birch	fender	Marks	sportscaster	
butter	Fern	Minister Sturm	squirm	
car	firm	modern	Star	
cart	first	morning	start	
charm	for	never	storm	
chore	forget	north	summer	
church	forgot	number	turn	
churn	girl	nurse	understand	
corn	hand	organist	whatever	
corner	harm	part	winter	
darn	harvest	pester	work	
dart	her	port	yarn	

2

GRAM AND
GRAMPS MARKS

Story Summary:

Pat and Trish Marks are driving to Wisconsin with their dad, Herbert, to visit his parents, who own a dairy farm. Gram and Gramps are excited about seeing their son and granddaughters. When they finish their morning chores, Gramps gives instructions for the day's work to his farmhand, Lester Sparks. Lester discovers that one of Gramps's prize pigs, Star, is giving birth to her piglets. Just then, Herbert and the girls arrive. The vet is called and everyone awaits her arrival.

 It is dark. Pat, Trish, and Dad are in the car. They will get to Gram and Gramps Marks' farm in the morning.

Gram and Gramps Marks live in the northwest corner of Wisconsin. Gramps tends his crops and stock. Gram helps Gramps with the chores and is the organist at the church, too. Gram darns the church linens for Minister Sturm.

Gramps has a big red brick barn in the back. He has a hundred tin milk cans in the barn. Gramps sells his milk to the man from the milk shop. Gram picks eggs from her hens to sell to the milk man, too.

The milk truck stops at Gramps's barn at six in the morning to pick up the milk

cans. At the milk shop, they can
churn milk and turn it into butter.

Gramps gets up with the sun
in the morning. Gramps's
farmhand, Lester Sparks,
helps Gramps tend the farm. Lester helps

Gram finish with the hens
and eggs.

Lester had come to the
farm to help Gramps with
the harvest. Whatever
Gramps had for him to do,
Lester could do it.

"Lester, I have got to have a quick bath. I
expect Herbert and the grandkids this
morning," Gramps said. "Get the corn shucks
and harvest scraps and cut them up for
mulch. You can stack up the mulch and cart
it to the north corner of the barn when you
finish."

"I will, Art. Should I check on the pigs in the storm shed, too? Your fat corn-fed pig, Star, could have her piglets this morning. If I am not with her to help her when they are born, some harm could come to Star's piglets."

Gramps said, "Thanks, Lester. Check her. I cannot think what I would do if I did not have you to help run this farm! Fern and I are just thinking of Herbert's trip with the kids in the car. It is a long, hard trip for them, and I will not rest until they are at the farm with us."

Art and Fern left Lester and went up the path and the porch steps to have a bath.

Mr. Marks was born on the farm. His dad

was born on the farm, too. Mr. Marks's granddad got

to Wisconsin as a lad and was the first to farm this land.

Art and Fern Marks were sad when Herbert left the farm to work for a big firm.

"Pat or Trish could farm this land," said Art to Fern. "They are girls, but modern girls can do whatever they want. Will Pat or Trish understand the thrill of the smell of rich, black dirt when plants start to pop up in the spring?"

"Art, the girls do not want to farm this land. Do not forget, Art, Pat plans to work as a sportscaster and Trish wants a job in the stock market. That Trish is a math whiz..."

"Art! Fern! Come quick!" Lester said. "Some of the piglets are sick. Star is having a fit. Help! Get the vet. Tell her to come to the farm. Tell her to come quick."

Just then, the girls ran into the backyard. "Gram! Gramps!" yelled Pat and Trish with a big hug and kiss.

Gramps said, "Herbert! Quick! Come to the storm shed. Some of Star's piglets are sick!"

When Dad got to the shed, Gramps said, "I am glad you have come. Can you give us a hand? Lester and I are helping Star with the piglets until the vet comes."

Gram and the girls went up the back path. "Pat, you run as fast as you can and  ring up the vet. The number is on the pad on the desk."

"I want to help, too, Gram," Trish said. "I wish I could help you with the canning, just as I did last summer. You are the best gram

in Wisconsin!" Trish had a big kiss for her gram.

"When will the vet come, Pat?" Gram said to Pat. "What did they tell you?"

"I got the vet's. They said that her car should get to the farm in just a bit," said Pat. Trish and Pat sat on the porch with Gram and helped her put up corn and jam for the church picnic.

When would the vet come? Trish just had to ask, "Do you think that Star's piglets will get better?"

Teacher/Parent Pages

Use the following questions to stimulate language growth, imagination, conceptual relationships, and higher-level thinking skills. These activities will encourage conversation and help develop language skills. Students must know that their ideas are important and that their questions will be heard. Have fun and accept all reasonable answers while praising and encouraging questioning from the students.

Vocabulary Expansion

Describe and define these words and phrases:

dairy farm	cattle	preparation
excitement	plow	milking machine
instruction	tractor	canning
await	contact	reminisce
arrival	mention	mulch

Language Expansion Activities

1. Get some books about farms and make a farm diorama with your reading group. How will you know whether or not it is authentic?

2. Make a list of at least five farm animals. With your friends, learn why farmers keep each kind of animal. Explain what the farmers have to do to take care of the animals.

Language Expansion Questions

1. Where did Gram and Gramps Marks live?

2. What season was it when the Markses drove to the farm?

3. What were the chores Gramps had Lester Sparks do for him? Check in the text and list them. Name other chores, not mentioned in the story, that Gramps might have had his farmhand do.

4. What happened to Star when the piglets were being born? Who did Gram contact to help Star?

5. What do you think will happen when the vet arrives? Why do people who keep animals have to be very careful with new animal babies?

6. Gram and Gramps were called other names. What did Mr. Marks call them? What did Lester call them? What other names do people call your own parents and grandparents? Explain why.

7. Pat and Trish are lucky to have grandparents. Do you have grandparents? If so, do they live far away, like the girls' grandparents in the story, or nearby? Write and/or tell about your grandparents. Draw a picture of them to illustrate your story.

8. Gram and Gramps had made preparations for Pat's and Trish's visit. When relatives visit you, what do you and your family do?

9. Gramps selected Lester to be his farmhand because he was a hard worker. Pretend that you are hiring someone to help you with your homework. What questions would you ask the person?

10. Gram was "putting up" corn and jam for the church picnic. What does that mean? Why is it important to help with events at your school, church, and other organizations?

11. Now that the year 2000 has come, we know that there are no limits to occupations for women or men. When the authors wrote, "They are girls, but modern girls can do whatever they want," exactly what did they mean? Do you think Pat or Trish might want to farm Gramps's land? What are some of the occupations women might choose in 2000 that they did not choose in 1900?

THE END OF SUMMER

UNIT 19

Phonology/Morphology Concepts

- If a syllable contains an **-r**, the /r/ phoneme controls the vowel phoneme.
  - There are three different **-r** controlled phonemes:
    1. /ar/ (car)
    2. /or/ (sort)
    3. /er/, /ir/, /ur/ (germ, sir, curt)
  - A syllable that ends with an **r-** controlled vowel is an **r-controlled syllable**.

Vocabulary

after	dirt	Herbert	porter	*come*
Art	escort	hornets	September	*some*
barn	far	Lester Sparks	short	*who*
bender	farm	market	spark	
birch	fender	Marks	sportscaster	
butter	Fern	Minister Sturm	squirm	
car	firm	modern	Star	
cart	first	morning	start	
charm	for	never	storm	
chore	forget	north	summer	
church	forgot	number	turn	
churn	girl	nurse	understand	
corn	hand	organist	whatever	
corner	harm	part	winter	
darn	harvest	pester	work	
dart	her	port	yarn	

14

THE END OF SUMMER

Story Summary:

Summer is over and Pat and Trish have to say good-bye to Gram and Gramps and to the farm. Their jet will leave soon, but there are a few things that the girls must do before leaving. Trish goes to say good-bye to Star and the piglets, and Pat has a conversation with Gramps. On the way to the airport, Gram and Gramps tell stories about Herbert, the girls' father, when he was a boy on the farm.

Herbert left the farm in midsummer. After Dad left, Pat and Trish got to visit with Gram and Gramps on the farm until September.

"Well," Gramps said to his grandkids, "I am sad that the end of summer has come. You girls charm us and spark us up. I cannot finish any chores when you are here!"

"Gramps, *you* are the man with the charm," said the girls with grins.

"Trish, you had best run in and get your Gram. Let's start the car, Pat. Your jet will have left," Gramps said to the girls.

"OK, Gramps," said Trish, "I will go get her."

Trish and Pat felt sad. September would mark the end of summer, long treks on the farm, and fishing with Gramps. They could not come back until winter.

Gramps and Pat went up the path to get the car.

"A trip to the farm helps me understand just what I want to do when I get big, Gramps," said Pat. "I want to farm this land just as you have."

"I am glad, Pat. Gram did not think that you would want to farm. But as I would catch you at your chores this summer, I could tell that you were as fond of farming as I am," Gramps said.

"Summer is just too short! I will miss you and this farm very much, Gramps," Pat said. "But I will be glad to be back with Dad, too. I miss him."

Trish ran up to Pat and Gramps. "You had better get your bags in the car, Pat. Gram is set to go," Trish said.

Pat ran to put her bags into the car. She was sad, but Dad had said that Tam and Kim would come with him to pick her up.

"Gramps," said Trish, "could I just run to the pigpen and have a last chat with Star and the piglets?" Trish was the one to nurse the piglets when they were sick. She did not think she could ever part with them.

"Go on, but be quick. We must get a start on," said Gramps. "And tell Lester not to  forget to shut the latch when the car gets past the dirt path."

At last they were in the car and Trish said to her sister, "Did you ever think

Dad would miss us this much? I miss Dad, too. I miss him a lot."

"Well, he never sent us as many letters as he did this summer," said Pat. "I do wish that he could have spent the last part of the summer here on the farm with us."

Gramps said, "You two girls are the best things Herbert has. After your mom was sick, when you were just tots, your Gram and I said you could come to the farm with us. But Herbert said, 'Whatever comes, I must think of the girls first.' "

"Gram, tell us what Dad did when he was just six," said Trish. "I think it is fun when you tell us the things Dad did back then."

"I cannot forget his first clash with a bunch of hornets. The hornets' nest was hidden in that big birch in the backyard," said Gram.

"Your dad sat up in that birch a lot, and the hornets had never stung him until that morning. I was yelling for him to get in the car for church when. . . PLOP! He fell from that birch and ran as fast as a dart. But the hornets were too fast and stung him bad. Your dad got sick from the stings. I must admit, your dad never felt as bad as that," Gram said.

"We will have to pester Dad with that yarn!" said Pat with a grin.

"Well, girls," said Gramps, "I will never forget Herbert's first fender-bender. The hot sparks from that car shot up to the top of the barn."

"Your dad was to escort some girl to the church picnic. Herbert was in a big rush. As your dad was backing up the car, there was a big crash. The car had hit the barn. First there were sparks. Oh, the barn did burn! Gram and I said that the barn would never stand up after such a shock!"

"But the barn is still there," Gram said. "And Gramps has got us here at last! You two have got to get on that jet quick."

Pat and Trish had big hugs for Gram and Gramps. As they ran up to the ramp, they said, "What a grand summer it was! You two are the best!"

Teacher/Parent Pages

Use the following questions to stimulate language growth, imagination, conceptual relationships, and higher-level thinking skills. These activities will encourage conversation and help develop language skills. Students must know that their ideas are important and that their questions will be heard. Have fun and accept all reasonable answers while praising and encouraging questioning from the students.

Vocabulary Expansion

Describe and define these words and phrases:

conversation	explosion	lonely
reminisce	church bazaar	reunited
airport	relate	relationship
baggage	relatives	pester
activities	responsibilities	yarn

Language Expansion Activities

1. Get a book from the library about hornets. Have your teacher or parent read it to you. Write a story about hornets' habits.

2. Draw/color/paint a picture of what the barn must have looked like when it burst into flames. Describe your picture to your friends. Make the noises the barn made while it was burning.

Language Expansion Questions

1. Why did Pat's and Trish's dad have to leave the farm before the girls did?

2. What were some of the fun activities they couldn't do in the city that Pat and Trish got to do on the farm? List them and add some more activities that you would like to do on a farm.

3. Tell the two stories that Gram and Gramps related to the girls about their dad when he was a boy.

4. What happened to Star and the piglets? How do you know?

5. The girls had to do chores for Gram and Gramps. Do you have to do chores at your house? What are they?

6. Pat and Trish were away from their dad for a long time. They had a great time on the farm, but they missed him a lot. Have you ever been away from your parent(s)? How did it feel?

7. Pat was sad to leave her grandparents. At the same time, she was happy to get back to her dad. Think of a time you have felt sad and happy at the same time. Explain the circumstances.

8. Gramps said that his granddaughters "charm us and spark us up." What did he mean by that? Do you know anyone who makes you feel that way? Tell or write about them.

9. What do you think this story tells us about grandparents and their relationships to their grandkids?

10. Describe how Trish felt when she had to say good-bye to Star and the piglets. Have you ever felt that way? Write about it.

SID NORTH

UNIT 20

Phonology/Morphology Concepts

- An open syllable is a syllable that **ends** with a vowel (an open phoneme).
- Open syllables have long vowel sounds.
- A long vowel sounds the same as the letter that represents it.

Vocabulary

be	no	*once*
go	she	*very*
he	so	*whose*
hero	we	
Hi	zero	
me		

SID NORTH

Story Summary:

Sid North is an excellent math student. Pat Marks is great at sports, but she has a hard time with math. One afternoon, Pat suggests to Sid that she go to his house after soccer so that he can help her with math. Sid hesitates because he knows that there are bad people around his neighborhood, and he does not want Pat to get hurt. He thinks about his mother and the hard times she has had raising Sid and his younger brother, Hi. Finally, he tells Pat the truth and suggests that she ask her father to drive her to his home so she will be safe. But Pat's dad has other ideas.

Sid North is smart. His best subject is math. Pat is best in sports. She wants to be a sportscaster or a farmer, but math is very hard for her.

"Sid, I did so bad on the last math test, I cannot tell Dad," Pat said. "If I could go to your flat after the soccer match, you could help me. I just do not understand math. Could you help me after soccer?"

Sid said to himself, "I should tell Pat she cannot come." Sid's mom could not get a job

and she did not have much cash. They had a flat on Birch Lane. Whenever she could, Sid's mom would help a yard man trim shrubs. But that was just in summer.

Once, when Sid was just a toddler, Mrs. North had a job at a dress shop, but after Hi was born, she got very sick. When she got well, the dress shop had shut forever.

Mrs. North was upset that Sid and Hi had torn shirts and pants. She said to herself, "I wish I could get Sid and Hi some shirts, but I cannot. I will just have to mend the things they have."

Sid felt bad. "Pat," he said, "could you get your dad to bring you? We live on Birch Lane and they sell drugs on the corner. You could get hurt if you come over. Could your dad bring you? Mom will not let Hi or me do anything unless she comes with us. Just tell your dad to honk his horn and Mom will come to get you."

"Dad can do that," Pat said. "Thanks a lot, Sid. We will come after the soccer match."

Once, last summer, Pat had invited Sid over for a swim. When Sid got to Pat's, he said to himself, "Wow! What a super pad! Pat must get whatever she wants."

A long path led up to Pat's front porch. Pat's dad had two cars. A big arch over the path was filled with pink and red buds.

Sid had never swum in a backyard. He had fun, yet he felt bad for his mom and Hi. "I will get this for Mom," Sid said.

Sid could not forget what he said to his mom when he got back from Pat's: "Mom, I am telling you. I will get a top-notch job when I get big. I will work hard and get you and Hi anything you want."

Pat's dad said to her, "Pat, I do not want you to go to Sid's. Let Sid come and do math with you."

"But admit it, Dad," she said, "you said to Trish and me that we should be pals with kids no matter what they had. If they did not have anything, it did not matter. You said we should help kids that are hard up.

"Do not forget, Dad. Sid is helping me. I am the kid whose math is bad, not Sid."

"I will admit that I said that to you and Trish," Dad said. "But understand me, Pat. Drugs can do bad things. I am your dad and I have to think of you first."

"Well, what if you come with me? Sid's mom will come to get me, and she will be with us until you come back for me."

"No. I do not want you to go."

"Just this once, Dad? I will never ask for anything else."

"This is not the best plan. But I will let you go just this once," Dad said.

"Thanks, Dad!" said Pat.

Pat got into her dad's car. He was muttering. In the car, Mr. Marks was stern with Pat when she would start to chat. Just as they got to the corner of Birch Lane, Mr. Marks said, "Pat, I cannot do this. We are going back."

"Stop the car!" Pat said.

"No," said Mr. Marks, "and do not order  me to do anything. I am your dad. I have to do what is best for you."

"But what will Sid think, Dad?"

"I will go back and pick up Sid. But you are not to go."

"But!" said Pat.

"We will not discuss this any further."

Just as Pat and Sid were going to finish the last of the math chapter, Dad went in to chat with them.

Sid said to him, "Mr. Marks, I can understand what you did. I was thinking that Pat should not come myself. But I did not want to tell her. Pat is a fantastic girl. She could be hurt. Some thug could mug her. I am not upset that you did not let her come," Sid said to Mr. Marks.

Mr. Marks said, "Sid, you are smart and I am fond of you. If I can ever help you, just ask. A kid like you should get as much help as he can. You will go far."

Teacher/Parent Pages

Use the following questions to stimulate language growth, imagination, conceptual relationships, and higher-level thinking skills. These activities will encourage conversation and help develop language skills. Students must know that their ideas are important and that their questions will be heard. Have fun and accept all reasonable answers while praising and encouraging questioning from the students.

Vocabulary Expansion

Describe and define these words and phrases:

suggest	mug	debate
hesitate	unsafe	defiant
neighborhood	change your mind	hard up
drugs	bad idea	tutor
thug	bad luck	unfortunate

Language Expansion Activities

1. Describe your neighborhood. Is it safe? How do you know? Draw a picture of your neighborhood and some of the people who live there.

2. What is your best subject? Take turns teaching each other something new, or something you are learning in school. Help a younger brother, sister, or friend with homework. Then explain to your group exactly what you did to help.

Language Expansion Questions

1. What was Sid's best subject?

2. Pat was best in sports. What did she say that she wanted to be when she grew up?

3. Why didn't Sid want Pat to come to his house?

4. How did Sid's mom feel about living on Birch Lane? How do you know?

5. Why did Pat get into an argument with her dad?

6. Drugs are harmful to people. Do you have a drug education program in your school? If so, what have you learned in the program? If not, would you like to learn more about what drugs can do to harm people? Write a letter to your principal, explaining how you feel about having or not having a drug education program in your school.

7. What did Pat and Sid learn from their experience?

8. Do you think Pat's dad was right not to let her go to Sid's? Have your parents ever had to make a decision that you did not like or agree to? Tell about it.

9. Suppose that Pat's dad had let her go to Sid's to study. How could the story have been different?

10. Look at the line on the last page of the story that says "We will not discuss this any further." Who is speaking? How do you know?

GO, CATS, GO

UNIT 20

Phonology/Morphology Concepts

- An open syllable is a syllable that **ends** with a vowel (an open phoneme).
- Open syllables have long vowel sounds.
- A long vowel sounds the same as the letter that represents it.

Vocabulary

be	no	*once*
go	she	*very*
he	so	*whose*
hero	we	
Hi	zero	
me		

GO, CATS, GO

Story Summary:

One afternoon during a soccer game between the Jasper Cats and their archrivals, the Red Hornets, a teenager named Bo begins heckling the fans and members of the Hornets team. Jack Turner, Tam's older brother, is on the team with Dan Burger, an excellent soccer player who has a chance for a scholarship to Rutgers University. Sam, Sid, Mat, Tam, and some other kids are sitting in the stands with older students from the high school. At first, they think Bo is funny. But eventually, he shows his true colors and they discover that he is just a jerk.

The fans sat in the stands. They were all yelling for the Jasper Cats. *"Go, Cats, Go! Go, Cats, Go! Go, Cats, Go!"*

When Sam got back from the hot dog stand, he could tell the score from the numbers on the cards the man held up. The Red Hornets were winning, 2 to 1. He sat down to watch the rest of the match with Mat and Sid. Who would win? The Cats or the Red Hornets? Tam Turner felt bad. She said, "Hi, Sam. If we could just win this match, we could be champs."

Sam, Mat, and Sid were glum, too. The kids were big fans of the Jasper Cats. Tam said, "I am thinking of Jack. He and Dan and the rest of

them want so much to go on and be in the contest for district champs!"

Hornet fans had come to Jasper on a very big bus to watch the match. The Red Hornets had on red soccer shorts, long red socks, and black T-shirts with big red hornets on them.

A Jasper fan, Bo Vonert, was yelling at the Hornets. He was yelling things like, "Did your mom wash your soccer shorts? You can't win this soccer match! The Cats will rip you to shreds! Come up in the stands and get me!"

At first, the kids would grin when Bo would yell, "Kill the ref! Get back on your bus! The Cats will chomp your red bugs!"

But Sam said to Mat and Tam, "Remember what we said when we lost the

last match at the end of the summer? We said we would *never* be bad sports."

When Bo was yelling from the stands, Jack and Dan kept looking up at him. But Bo kept it up. He did not stop, even when Mr. Miller went into the stands. Mr. Miller had said, "You have got to stop this, Bo. This is not the kind of conduct we permit from Jasper fans."

Just then, Dan Burger's kick hit the net. The fans in the stands got up and yelled, *"Go, Dan! Go, Dan! Go, Cats, Go! Chomp the Bugs!"* The cards said Hornets 2, Cats 2.

The star of the Jasper Cats was Dan Burger. Dan was short and fast. He could zap the soccer net hard when he would kick.

The Cats had a plan. They would pass to Dan so he could kick. If they  could win this match, they could be district champs!

Dan and his dad had a visit from a man whose job was to pick the very best kicker for the Rutgers soccer club. The man had come to watch Dan and the Cats in the match with the Red Hornets.

As the game began, Dan had said to himself, "If I do well in this game, I could have a chance to go to Rutgers. Dad and Mom cannot send me there, so I will have to do well. I want to go to Rutgers!"

But the Cats were not winning. Dan, Jack, and the rest of them sat at the lockers. Mr. Fell was telling them, "You can win it.

Do your best. We still have the rest of the match to go. This will be the plan. . . ."

The band was marching, and the kids got hot dogs from the vendors in the stands.

As the Cats ran back on the soccer turf, the Jasper fans began to yell, *"Go, Cats, Go! Go, Cats, Go! Go, Cats, Go!"*

Bo Vonert would not let up. He kept on yelling. "Put the Hornet fans back on the bus! Go back to the hornet nest! We will zap your stingers!" Bo was a bad sport. Kim, Tam, Sid, Mat, and Sam had had it with Bo.

Tam said, "You should stop it, Bo. Jack and Dan and the Cats cannot think when you are yelling. Mr. Miller said you should stop. We want you to stop, too."

Mat was mad. "The Cats want to win. It is the big match, Bo. We could have a chance to be champs! So stop it!" Mat said.

"Shut up, short stuff! I will do whatever I want!" Bo picked up a rock to toss it at Mat, but the rock shot past the stands and onto the turf. A gasp sprang up from the stands. As the rock hit Dan in the shin, he fell with a start. He could not get up. Mr. Fell ran onto the turf to help Dan.

Dan was the hero of the Cats. With Dan, they had a chance to be champs. If Dan could not kick, what would Mr. Fell and the Cats do?

Teacher/Parent Pages

Use the following questions to stimulate language growth, imagination, conceptual relationships, and higher-level thinking skills. These activities will encourage conversation and help develop language skills. Students must know that their ideas are important and that their questions will be heard. Have fun and accept all reasonable answers while praising and encouraging questioning from the students.

Vocabulary Expansion

Describe and define these words and phrases:

archrival	true colors	hero
fan	jerk	coach
heckler	bad sport	principal
scholarship	rude comments	scorecards
eventually	cheerleader	district champ

Language Expansion Activities

1. Pretend that you are a cheerleader. Make up two cheers that you could get the crowd to yell. Write them down and practice them with your reading group.

2. Dan wished that he could get into Rutgers University on a scholarship. Do you have any wishes? Write about them.

Language Expansion Questions

1. Who was the star of the Jasper Cats?

2. When the story began, what was the score of the game?

3. Bo Vonert made some rude remarks to the Hornet fans. At first, the kids thought Bo was funny, but his rude comments got to be too much. Why did they change their minds about Bo's behavior? Do you know anyone who is rude?

4. Make a list of all the main events in the story. Go back into the text to make sure they are in order.

5. A soccer match is even more exciting when the score of the game is tied. The score was tied at the end of the story. Make up a new ending telling who won the match. How did the fans feel at the end of the game?

6. Dan is a great soccer player. But he didn't become great overnight. Tell how a person becomes very good at a sport.

7. The story says that Dan was a hero. Do you have any heroes? How could someone become a hero?

8. What do you think will happen to Bo? What would you do to him if you were the principal or the coach of the team? Why do you think Bo acted the way he did?

9. Name the character in the story that you would most like to be. Why?

10. At the end of the story, the fans were really let down because of what Bo did to Dan. Have you ever been let down by someone or something that you could not control? Write or tell about it.

DAN BURGER

UNIT 21

Phonology/Morphology Concepts

- Phoneme control by the final silent **-e:**
  - A vowel phoneme is long in a **vc + -e** word (end word pattern: vowel + consonant + **-e**).
  - Short vowel phonemes in **cvc** words become long vowel phonemes when **-e** is added at the end of a word (internal word pattern: consonant + vowel + consonant).
  - A syllable that ends with a final silent **-e** is a final **silent -e syllable**.

Vocabulary

advice	home	Mrs. Rame	spoke	*Dr.*
bake	homemade	name	state	*from*
bone	hope	nine	strive	*give*
broke	joke	Pine Lane	take	*here*
cake	Kole	ride	tale	*live*
came	lake	rule	tape	
chime	lame	sake	time	
close	late	same	use	
face	life	score	wave	
fine	like	sideline	while	
five	made	skate	wife	
game	make	slide		
grade	more	smile		

DAN BURGER

Story Summary:

Dan Burger is the star of the Jasper Cats, the high school soccer team. He is at home recuperating from a leg injury he received in last week's district championship soccer game. His team has won and will play in the state finals, but Dan will not get to play and he is crushed. He receives many cards and letters, but the second grade soccer stars help him more than anyone else.

Dan Burger was the hope of the Cats. He was the star. He could kick, slide, and pass to the net better than the rest.

When a rock hit Dan in the shin during the game for district champs, he felt its sting. He fell and could not get up. A sportscaster said that Dan would be taken to the bone clinic for tests. After that, Dan did not remember much.

When the district game came to an end, the score was Hornets 2, Cats 3. Jack Turner had scored for the Cats. The Cats had made it to the game for state champs, but the Cats would not have Dan.

At first, Dr. Kole said Dan could be in the game for the state champs. But after he got Dan's tests back, Dr. Kole said that it was more than just a fine crack.

Dan would be in a
full-leg cast for a long time.
He would limp. Dr. Kole
had to give him a crutch.
Dan would have to sit on
the sidelines while the Cats
were in the game for state
champs.

Dan tried not to think about it, but as he
got up from his bed at the clinic, he felt mad
and sad for himself. He was very upset. He
could not help but think his hopes to get into
Rutgers were lost.

But once he got into his dad's car for the
ride home, he remembered the things he
could still do with his life. There were the
Kit-Cats. Dan had a smile on his face as he
remembered his grade two pals.

He could still give his time to the grade
two soccer stars. He never made fun of the

Kit-Cats when he helped them with kicking and passing into the net. Dan gave them many hints on the game.

Still, Dan could not help thinking, "I could be lame for life. I will not have funds to go to Rutgers unless this leg mends."

Dan and his dad drove home to Pine Lane. His dad and mom had a bake shop in the back. Mrs. Burger had just put five cakes in to bake. As they drove up, she said, "Here you are! Hi, Dan! You have more cards and gifts here than you did at the clinic! Can I have a big hug from my star?"

Just then, some kids came up on the back porch. Five grade two soccer

kids had homemade gifts for Dan. Dan was in the den watching TV. As Carlos, Sis, Dick, Trish, and Bud came into the den, a smile came to Dan's face. "Hi, Kit-Cats," said Dan. "What's up? I am glad you have come. Do you have a munchkin joke for me?"

"Well, Dan," said Bud, "we had a joke for you, but the joke was on us. We lost the game with the Pink Hornets." Bud did not want to tell Dan that they had lost, but he had to.

Carlos spoke up, "We did not do too well, Dan. In fact, we lost zip to five. It was a big bust. What should we do, Dan?"

"Well," said Dan, "do not get so upset when you do not win. You have to want to win, and you will. Just strive to do your best. You have to think of the games to come and never give up hope. Winning is doing your best. You are winners!"

"Thanks, Dan," the munchkins chimed.

Mrs. Burger came in and gave them some milk and cake from her bake shop.

Bud, Dick, and Carlos gave Dan the gift. In a big box was a soccer turf with a net. "Mrs. Rame let us do it for an art project," said Trish and Sis with red faces.

"It's perfect," Dan said. "I will put it on the shelf in the den so that I can think of you kids. You munchkins are the big stars."

As the munchkins got up to go, Mr. Burger said, "My wife and I are glad you came. Dan likes you so much. It helps when you come to visit him."

"Dan's the best," sang the munchkins, cake still on their lips.

Then Dan sat and started to think.

"Dad and Mom," said Dan, "the munchkins did not win the grade two game while I was at the clinic. They felt bad. I said they could win, even when they had lost. But that should be a rule I live for, too. I am the one who should take that advice!"

"Dan," said his dad, "you had a bit of bad luck. Your mom and I understand. You will do what it takes to get over this."

Dan gave his mom and dad hugs. "With your help, I think I can!" said Dan.

They had the rest of the cake and milk.

Teacher/Parent Pages

Use the following questions to stimulate language growth, imagination, conceptual relationships, and higher-level thinking skills. These activities will encourage conversation and help develop language skills. Students must know that their ideas are important and that their questions will be heard. Have fun and accept all reasonable answers while praising and encouraging questioning from the students.

Vocabulary Expansion

Describe and define these words and phrases:

recuperating	X rays	last chance
cast	bone clinic	volunteer
fine crack	full-leg cast	scholarship
crushed	crutches	bakery
homemade gifts	commiserate	pep talk

Language Expansion Activities

1. Have you ever thought of helping someone else with a subject or sport you are good at? Tell about what you could help others do. Write a plan to help others, and make a list of the ways you could help them.

2. What kind of gift would you have made for Dan if you had been his friend? Prepare a set of directions with drawings. Be sure the directions are in order. Then explain to a friend how to make it. Make one for a sick friend or relative.

Language Expansion Questions

1. What happened to Dan Burger?

2. Where was Dan when the story began?

3. Who came to pick Dan up? Where did they go?

4. When Dan got home, what did his mother say and do? Explain how Dan's mom and dad were feeling.

5. Who came to visit Dan? What did they bring him?

6. Dan felt mad and sad about being hurt. What were some of his reasons for feeling that way? Have you ever felt that way? Explain how you felt and why.

7. Dan was a volunteer. He coached the Kit-Cats on weekends. Have you ever volunteered for anything? Why is it good to be a volunteer?

8. The grade two soccer players were upset and depressed about losing their game. Dan gave them some good advice. Look back in the text and read the advice Dan gave them. Why was it such good advice?

9. The kids visited Dan because he was recuperating and could not leave home. Have you ever visited anyone who was too injured or ill to go out? Tell about your experience.

10. At the end of the story, Dan told his parents that he should take his own advice. Have you ever given anyone advice that you should have taken yourself? Can you explain why people may not take their own advice?

SEPTEMBER TALES

UNIT 21

Phonology/Morphology Concepts

- Phoneme control by the final silent **-e:**
  - A vowel phoneme is long in a **vc + -e** word (end word pattern: vowel + consonant + **-e**).
  - Short vowel phonemes in **cvc** words become long vowel phonemes when **-e** is added at the end of a word (internal word pattern: consonant + vowel + consonant).
  - A syllable that ends with a final silent **-e** is a final **silent -e syllable**.

Vocabulary

advice	home	Mrs. Rame	spoke	*Dr.*
bake	homemade	name	state	*from*
bone	hope	nine	strive	*give*
broke	joke	Pine Lane	take	*here*
cake	Kole	ride	tale	*live*
came	lake	rule	tape	
chime	lame	sake	time	
close	late	same	use	
face	life	score	wave	
fine	like	sideline	while	
five	made	skate	wife	
game	make	slide		
grade	more	smile		

SEPTEMBER
TALES

Story Summary:

It was the first day of school for the gang. They were now in junior high. The students had lots to talk about—their new school and new teachers and friends. But in the background, they could hear sirens. As they were meeting their new teacher, the fire engines haunted them until . . .

It was the first of September and the gang came back to school with many tales of summer events.

Names were taped on the desks. As they sat, many of them were thinking that they would miss Miss Pitt. Kim and Mat waved as Tam came in.

Far off, they could detect something like a fire truck. Nick got up from his desk.

"Sit at your desks, kids," Ms. Silver said as she came in, "and let's chat for a while." She had a smile for the class. "I have some rules that you must observe, and if you do, we will have a fine year. I am here to help you. If you do not understand something, just tell me. I expect you to do your best. We can make this the very best class ever!"

Once more, they were distracted. The horns broke the stillness of school. They were closer. The kids felt restless. . . .

Ms. Silver picked up the list of names from her desk. "Nick Hopkins, tell us what you did this summer."

"Well," said Nick, "I had a chance to be in a rock band while the sax man was sick. Then once in late June, I had a gig with a jazz band at the lake. That was the best thing I did!"

"Splendid, Nick!" said Ms. Silver. She went on. "Where is Pat Marks?"

"Here I am, Ms. Silver," said Pat as she put up her hand.

"Well, Pat," said Ms. Silver, "what was your summer like?"

"We went to Wisconsin last summer to be with Gram and Gramps," Pat said with a grin. "We had fun, but we worked hard, too. Gramps's prize pig, Star, had piglets. We had to get the vet to help. The piglets were OK, but it upset the farm for a while."

"Once, we sang some Rat Pack songs for Gram. But Gramps said he didn't like that hard rock stuff!" The class snickered.

Next, Ms. Silver asked, "What did you do this summer, Al?"

Tam and Nick were distracted. "That fire truck is even closer," Tam said.

"Well, Ms. Silver," said Al, "I didn't have a job, but I invented some new games and programs for my computer!"

"It's fine to have a whiz kid like you in the class," Ms. Silver said. "And I  could use some help on my computer, too!"

Tam's turn was next. Ms. Silver asked what her summer was like.

"Well," Tam said, "summer was OK. I got to skate two times with Kim and Pat. But I had to sit at home with the twins and Sis. Once, we went to the shore when Dad had time off. We had a super time crabbing and swimming. But I wish I had had more time to spend with the gang. I never had much time to do the things I wanted."

"When I was a girl, we had six kids, too, Tam," Ms. Silver said, "and I was the eldest. So I understand!"

Sam's turn came next. "What was your summer like, Sam?" asked Ms. Silver.

"My summer was the best," said Sam. "I had a job at a pet shop. I like pets, so the job was a snap."

"Super, Sam! Can you tell us what you did, Sid? Are you the math whiz?"

"I like math, for sure, Ms. Silver. . ."

Just then, fire trucks went past. Horns were blasting and the kids jumped up.

"There is a fire at Lake School. The fire trucks are going to the school. Do not panic." Mr. Blake was on the intercom.

Then the kids started yelling, "Fire at Lake School!" The kids went to Lake School until the end of sixth grade.

"Sis!" Tam let out a shrill yell.

Pat was very upset. "Trish cannot run as fast as Sis!" she said.

What if Bud gets left at his desk?" said Nick. "He just can't get left!"

"Stop it!" yelled Ms. Silver. "Sit here at your desks. Do not panic."

They did as Ms. Silver said, but they could not think of anything but the kids at Lake School.

As they left Ms. Silver's class to go to math, they whispered to themselves. A hush put an end to the panic. They were scared.

Would the kids be OK? Would any kids be hurt? Miss Pitt was at Lake School. So was Bud. So was Trish. So was Sis. . . .

Teacher/Parent Pages

Use the following questions to stimulate language growth, imagination, conceptual relationships, and higher-level thinking skills. These activities will encourage conversation and help develop language skills. Students must know that their ideas are important and that their questions will be heard. Have fun and accept all reasonable answers while praising and encouraging questioning from the students.

Vocabulary Expansion

Describe and define these words and phrases:

junior high school	orchestra	comprehend
adventures	snicker	eldest
uncomfortable	invention	intercom
diversion	inventor	blaring
roster	whiz kid	uncertain

Language Expansion Activities

1. Pretend that you are trying to talk to others in the class and sirens begin blaring outside. Discuss what it is like to have to talk and listen with that kind of distraction.

2. Draw a picture of what you think Lake School looked like after this story. Write a new story to go along with your picture.

Language Expansion Questions

1. In what season did this story take place? How do you know?

2. What was the new teacher's name? Describe her. Do you think you would like her? Why?

3. What did Ms. Silver ask each student to do for her? Has anyone ever asked you to tell about your summer vacation? How did you feel about that?

4. If you could have been any character in the story, who would you have been for the summer? Why?

5. Tam said that her summer had been somewhat good and somewhat bad. She had to baby-sit every day, but she did get to go out with her friends sometimes. Have you ever had a day or season that was good and bad? Describe it. Explain how something can be good and bad at the same time.

6. As the students were speaking, what was distracting them in the background? Why? How do you think they were feeling?

7. Think of a time you have been distracted by something. What was it? How did it end? Why is it sometimes hard to concentrate?

8. Ms. Silver said that she could understand how Tam felt. Why do you think she could understand Tam's feelings?

9. When Mr. Blake came on the intercom and told the students about the fire, some of them panicked. Explain why some people might have trouble staying calm. Why is staying calm important?

10. What would be a good sequel to this story? Write it.

THE FIRE

UNIT 22

Syllable Concepts

- Each vowel phoneme creates a separate **syllable**.
- To count the number of syllables in a word, listen for and mark each separate vowel phoneme.
- To divide words into syllables, use these guidelines:
  - **vccv** words (pattern: vowel + consonant + consonant + vowel), divide between the consonants.
  - **vcv** words (pattern: vowel+consonant+vowel), divide after the first vowel if the vowel phoneme is **long**.
  - Divide **vcv** words after the consonant if the vowel phoneme is **short**.
  - Or if the vowel phoneme is **r-** controlled.
  - Divide **vcccv** words after the first of the three consonants.

Vocabulary

absent	corner	harder	silent	*want*
after	darker	insect	silver	
basket	dentist	invite	tennis	
became	depart	market	traffic	
become	dinner	never	until	
before	Elmer	open	update	
begin	forgot	panic	upon	
beside	gather	paper	vacate	
blanket	hamster	picnic	whisper	
cannot	happen	prevent		

THE FIRE

Story Summary:

On the first day of school, Ms. Elmer's second graders have just begun writing when the fire alarm rings. As they reach the exit, they realize that there is a real fire. Sis and Trish worry about the two hamsters left in their classroom. Students and teachers all gather behind Lake School and wait for instructions from their principal, Mr. Ade.

Carlos Corzo had just come to Lake School. Last summer, he had met Bud and Dick at soccer. They were on the Kit-Cats.

Ms. Elmer's grade two students whispered until she came into the class.

"I am Ms. Elmer. I am glad to have you in my class. On these papers, I want you to tell me some things you like to do," she said as she passed the papers to the students.

They became silent as they put names on the papers. She added, "I will not grade spelling on this paper. Just think of some interesting things you would like to tell us."

Bud did not like school. He had had a hard time during first grade, and he felt that grade two would be much harder. In the summer, he had so much fun he began to forget school. He stared at his blank paper.

Just then, the bell rang for a fire drill. Bud popped up. He said to Carlos, "Come on. You can line up beside me. We will have to be quiet until the last bell rings to tell us the drill is over. We cannot run." Ms. Elmer's class was quick to 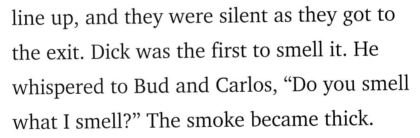 line up, and they were silent as they got to the exit. Dick was the first to smell it. He whispered to Bud and Carlos, "Do you smell what I smell?" The smoke became thick.

When they got past the exit, the classes lined up in the yard behind the school. Students whispered. This was no drill. This was a fire! Ms. Elmer asked Miss Pitt, "What do you think we should do?"

"Well, Mr. Ade will tell us what he wants us to do," she said. But Miss Pitt's smile was missing.

Trish started to sob. "My lunch box is inside, and the hamsters Ms. Elmer got for us. We want to save them!"

Some big kids were joking, "No more  school! No more homework! No more tests!" They acted like the fire was a gift.

Sis and Trish said to them, "You cannot make a joke of this. Ms. Elmer got some hamsters for us. They are inside, and we just have to save them."

A big kid said, "What if you ask Thad to get them? He helps kids in this school."

A hush came over the students as six more fire trucks drove up. Mr. Ade led them to the far back corner of the schoolyard.

 Then the big kids began to panic. Fire hoses were pumping as fast as they could, but flames were still popping.

Sis and Trish began to smile. Sis had spotted Thin Thad as he came near their line with the two hamsters. Ms. Elmer's class yelled, "Thanks, Thad!" Thad was a hero. He had saved their hamsters.

Then Thad reported to Mr. Ade, "I checked the classes. The entire school is vacated." The students yelled and clapped.

Mr. Ade was glad that his students were safe, but as he gazed at his school, he said to himself, "What should I do? I have more than 300 students to think of. And what of the students' files, the desks, and the other things in this school? Are they gone? Can we save anything?"

A traffic jam began to form. Moms and dads wanted to pick up kids. But before they left the yard, the students had to check with Ms. Elmer. She kept a list of her students, and she updated it as they left.

Sis's mom, Mrs. Turner, said to Ms. Elmer, "I am taking Sis, and I will take Trish Marks home with me, too. I have spoken to her dad."

"Mom, Ms. Elmer, can we take the hamsters home with us?" Sis and Trish begged. "Ms. Elmer got them for the class and Thad saved them from the fire. We want to take care of them until we come back to school. Can we?"

It was a long time before the fire trucks departed. When morning came, Mr. Ade, Miss Pitt, Ms. Elmer, and the rest of the staff gathered at Lake School. It was time to save the things they could, and to make plans for what to do next.

When they met that morning, Miss Pitt spotted a black lunch box beside the back exit. She gazed at Ms. Elmer.

"A lot of your life was in that school," Miss Pitt said. "Mine, too." They had never felt so sad.

Teacher/Parent Pages

Use the following questions to stimulate language growth, imagination, conceptual relationships, and higher-level thinking skills. These activities will encourage conversation and help develop language skills. Students must know that their ideas are important and that their questions will be heard. Have fun and accept all reasonable answers while praising and encouraging questioning from the students.

Vocabulary Expansion

Describe and define these words and phrases:

interesting	hazardous	assemble
fire drill	assignment	eventually
firefighter	await	hamster
school staff	smoke alarm	calm
safety precaution	sprinkler system	custodian

Language Expansion Activities

1. Locate a map which gives fire drill instructions for the students in your class. Examine the map carefully, and then write a list of directions for your class. Be certain that your written directions exactly match the instructions on the map.

2. Phone the fire station near your school. Request information about fire prevention at home and at school. Then, write a letter to the families of students in your school giving them information which they need to make their homes safe from fire. Explain the importance of fire safety to students outside your class.

Language Expansion Questions

1. What were the students doing at the beginning of the story?

2. How did Bud feel about school? Why?

3. During the summer, Bud and his friend Dick played on the soccer team with a new person in the neighborhood. Who was he? What did you learn about him in the story?

4. Who was their new teacher? Describe her. Tell some of the things she did and said in the story. What kind of person do you think she is? Do you think the students will like her? Why?

5. Describe what happened when the alarm went off. Was the students' behavior like the behavior of your own class when there is a fire drill? Why is behavior so important during a fire drill?

6. Trish and Sis were worried about something that they had left in the classroom. What was it and why were they so worried?

7. After all the students were lined up outdoors, Thad did something very heroic. What was it? What kind of man was Thad?

8. If you were a principal and your school had a fire, what would you have to think about? What might you have to replace? Make a list of all of the things you would have to consider.

9. Discuss all of the possible ways for the children's education to continue. What did the faculty talk about at the meeting?

10. There are many ways to improve fire safety. Discuss them. Why are some more important than others?

Unit 22, Book 2

AFTER THE FIRE

UNIT 22

Syllable Concepts

- Each vowel phoneme creates a separate **syllable**.
- To count the number of syllables in a word, listen for and mark each separate vowel phoneme.
- To divide words into syllables, use these guidelines:
  - **vccv** words (pattern: vowel + consonant + consonant + vowel), divide between the consonants.
  - **vcv** words (pattern: vowel+consonant+vowel), divide after the first vowel if the vowel phoneme is **long**.
  - Divide **vcv** words after the consonant if the vowel phoneme is **short**.
  - Or if the vowel phoneme is **r-** controlled.
  - Divide **vcccv** words after the first of the three consonants.

Vocabulary

absent	corner	harder	silent	*want*
after	darker	insect	silver	
basket	dentist	invite	tennis	
became	depart	market	traffic	
become	dinner	never	until	
before	Elmer	open	update	
begin	forgot	panic	upon	
beside	gather	paper	vacate	
blanket	hamster	picnic	whisper	
cannot	happen	prevent		

AFTER THE FIRE

Story Summary:

After a fire at Lake School, Mr. Ade, the principal, meets with the teachers and parents. They make plans to repair the school. Many people offer their help, but there is not enough money to replace the materials that are lost. They need a large donation if Lake School is to reopen. In the end, a surprise donor comes forth from the community. The children learn how important Lake School is to them.

 After the fire trucks left, many of the staff felt hopeless. But Mr. Ade said, "The fire is over, but Lake School is not. Together, we will renovate Lake School."

They had met at the home of Trish's dad, Herbert Marks, to make plans to renovate Lake School.

"We have a big job to do," Mr. Ade said to them when they met to draft the plans. "Some of the desks and other things are fine, but some of them were burned in the fire. We have to make a list of the things we must get before we can reopen.

"The biggest problem is that we are short on cash. It will cost a lot to replace the things that we have lost. I wish I could give you a better report."

The staff had concerns. They asked Mr. Ade things that he could not tell them.

"The first thing we must do is relocate the students. We want to fit them into classes in district schools. Ms. Rampart, the superintendent, wants to help us, but she must have help.

"Ms. Elmer, I will put you in charge of finding spots for students in grades K-3. Miss Pitt, you will work with Ms. Elmer and Ms. Rampart to find spots for the 4-6 graders." Mr. Ade went on to report the rest of his plan to the staff.

Mr. Marks wanted to be in charge of procuring funds to replace the things that had to be replaced. Many of the moms and dads said they would be glad to help him.

"Mr. Ade, we are behind you and your staff in the effort to renovate Lake School," said Mr. Marks.

"Mert Webster, Sam Webster, and many of Sam's pals have begun to pick up and sort what was left in the classes," Mr. Marks added. "Sam and his pals went to Lake School until they were in the sixth grade, and they want to help the school, too."

"Thanks, Herb. You and I can work with Mert." Mr. Ade was glad to have such fine help.

Mrs. Turner said, "We are planning a bake sale to help us to get things we must have before we can reopen Lake School."

"Bake sales are fine, but it is time to add up costs," Mr. Hopkins said. "We can never hope to reopen until we admit that we must have more cash. We can forget it unless we find a donor." A hush  came over them. It was a vast problem.

Nell Pitt had asked Jen Wells if her shop and the rest of the shops at the dock would let Lake School hold the bake sale on the wide ramp beside the market at the dock. Chick, Pam, and Ted had helped set up for the sale.

Baskets of cakes and baked things were selling fast. The bake sale was a big hit.

Trish and Sis were helping Ms. Elmer. Trish said, "Dad told me that we will not be going to school together any more. You get to go to the school on the corner beside your home, but I have to go to Westside. No matter what we sell, we just do not have the cash to reopen." Both girls felt sad.

"I have never beheld so many muffins in my life," Mrs. Grunch muttered.

"Hi, Mrs. Grunch," said Sis. "We are having a bake sale. There was a fire at school. Before we can reopen, Mr. Ade has to get lots of cash. Did you want a cake?"

"Selling cakes will not open a school," said Mr. Grunch. "When I was a lad, we had a fire at school. I remember a man that helped us back in '36. Times were bad then. Where is this Mr. Ade of yours?"

Before long, Mr. Ade had more cash than he had ever wished for. They had a donor. It was fantastic. Mr. Grunch had saved Lake School!

As the flag slid up the pole, Miss Pitt remembered many students from her classes at Lake School. She was glad that there would be many more students and classes.

Trish and Sis held hands. Mr. Ade said, "Lake School is open once more and I think you have come to respect what your school stands for. I will never forget the work that you did to help us reopen."

"Just before we reenter the school, I would like to thank the man who made this happen. Mr. Grunch, I invite you to come and visit us at Lake School any time."

"Bravo! Mr. Grunch!" they yelled. For the first time, Mr. Grunch had a smile.

Teacher/Parent Pages

Use the following questions to stimulate language growth, imagination, conceptual relationships, and higher-level thinking skills. These activities will encourage conversation and help develop language skills. Students must know that their ideas are important and that their questions will be heard. Have fun and accept all reasonable answers while praising and encouraging questioning from the students.

Vocabulary Expansion

Describe and define these words and phrases:

donation	offer of help	short on cash
donor	assignment	procuring funds
repair	respect	superintendent
replace	renovate	district schools
bake sale	draft the plans	relocate

Language Expansion Activities

1. Mrs. Turner made plans for a bake sale. Imagine that you are planning a bake sale to help your school. Make a list of all the things you would need to do. Then, write a letter to parents asking for different kinds of donations and assistance.

2. When people cooperate, they can accomplish many things. Create a story about students who cooperate to accomplish something. Then, take parts and act out the story with the others in your group or class. Put on the play for the others.

Language Expansion Questions

1. Where was the meeting at the beginning of the story? Why?

2. What kind of report did Mr. Ade give the committee of parents and teachers? How do you think Mr. Ade was feeling?

3. Mat and his friends had gone to a new school. Why were they so eager to help raise funds to renovate their old school?

4. What instructions did Mr. Ade give the teachers? Why was their job so important? What problems did the teachers have?

5. Why is it important for parents to help their children's schools? What things can parents do to help a teacher or a school?

6. What kinds of baked goods do you think were sold at the dock? What baked item would you contribute to a bake sale at school?

7. During the bake sale, a surprise donor offered the help that Mr. Ade needed to begin renovating Lake School. Who was the donor? Why were the students and parents so surprised?

8. What had happened during his own childhood that might have made Mr. Grunch decide to help Lake School? Explain why we sometimes make decisions based on things that happen to us.

9. A proverb is a short saying that teaches a lesson. One proverb says: "Never judge a book by its cover." What could that proverb teach us about people?

10. Describe how Sis and Trish felt when the flag went up the flagpole at the end of the story. How would you have felt?

Unit 23, Book 1

MOLLY MANCHESTER

UNIT 23

Phonology/Orthography Concepts

- When **-y** occurs at the **end** of a word, it represents a long vowel sound.
- At the end of a one-syllable word, **-y** represents long /i/.
- At the end of a word with more than one syllable, **-y** represents long /e/.

Vocabulary

army	Molly	sorry	*pretty*
buddy	my	story	*there*
by	myself	study	*Tuesday*
candy	nasty	Suzy	*Wednesday*
cry	play	try	*where*
curly	plenty	ugly	
dry	pony	way	
funny	ruby	worry	
Lady	say		
lucky	simply		

MOLLY
MANCHESTER

Story Summary:

Molly Manchester has moved a lot because her dad is in the army. She has lived in many cities and towns all over the world. Molly has a horse named Lady, who is her best friend. Molly is used to having a hard time making new friends. This school proves to be no different. Pat tells the story of Molly Manchester to Trish when Trish meets a new friend.

Pat was telling Trish the story of Molly Manchester. "When Molly entered school this fall, Tam, Kim, and I were not very nice to her."

"We were not trying to be rude, but sometimes when kids go to a place for the first time, the kids who are there ignore them. And that's just what happened the first time we met Molly.

"She tried talking to Kim in math, but Kim just kept working problems. Tam and I would not ask Molly to study with us. But Molly didn't cry. She just kept trying to be

 nice. She was used to it. Last year she lived in Rome. Before that, she had lived in many different places. Her dad is in the army. He was in Desert Storm.

"Once, at lunch, Molly asked me, 'Can I sit with you, Pat?'

"I said, 'OK, but Tam and Kim sit here.' It was pretty rude, if I do say so myself.

"Later, after lunch, when Kim, Tam, and I were on the way to P.E. class, Tam just fell over.

"Kim started to cry. She was yelling, 'Tam! Tam! What's the matter?'

"Tam's face turned red, and she could not say anything. She was gasping and panting.

"Molly dashed up to us and said, 'Let me check her. I can do CPR. Get 911. Tell them Tam's face is flushed. She has choked on something. I will start CPR.'

"Kim ran to get Mr. Ade. I got 911, and Molly stayed with Tam and started CPR.

"By the time the medics got there, Tam felt better. CPR had worked. They had to take her to the Med Clinic, and her dad came to get her and take her home.

"That should have made us pals with Molly, but we still acted like she was ugly or something.

"When she went home that day, she sat on her bed and started to cry. 'Mom, I can't make pals at school. Why do they hate me so much?' Molly simply could not understand us.

" 'I think you just had a bad first try,' Molly's mom had told her. 'Maybe the girls will make you welcome the next time.' But it was no use. Molly went to ride her pony, Lady, and think. 'I bet if I could do just one more big favor, the girls would like me,' Molly said to Lady. Lady was the only one who was always there for Molly.

"Molly and Lady went for a long ride to try to forget things at school," Pat said. "It  was just at that same time when we lost Tam's mom's ruby ring. We were scared.

"Tam said to Kim and me, 'It's your mistake, too. We should not have done it.'

 " 'Don't blame us,' Kim fired back. 'You snatched the ruby ring from your mom's red velvet candy box.'

"At first, we were just going to play a funny prank on Tam," Pat said to Trish. "But it was no fun. If Tam's mom would find the ring missing, she would get mad. Tam, Kim, and I were plenty scared.

"We started to inspect the yard behind Tam's place. Just then, Molly rode up on

Lady. As Molly said 'hi' to us, Lady ate the grass and some clover in Tam's yard.

"We were telling Molly the sad tale and petting Lady's curly mane. Molly felt this was her big chance. She wanted to help us, but could she?

"Tam was in a panic. It was a crisis for us, too. I kept thinking Dad would kill me.

"We were sitting there worrying, but then we got lucky. When Lady's head came up, there was something red flashing on her nose! Lady had turned up the ring in the grass! We gave Lady and Molly a big hug.

" 'There's the ruby ring!' Molly said with a cry as the ring dropped back into the grass. Tam picked it up. She was in shock.

" 'You have saved my life for the second time, Molly! And I can put the ruby ring back in Mom's box, where it belongs! But you must think we are very nasty. We were just so upset about the ring,' said Tam.

"So we asked Molly to forgive us and be our pal! She was glad and so were we."

Pat said to Trish, "Just remember the story of Molly Manchester the next time Suzy wants to play with you and Sis. And if you blab this story to Dad, you have had it!"

Teacher/Parent Pages

Use the following questions to stimulate language growth, imagination, conceptual relationships, and higher-level thinking skills. These activities will encourage conversation and help develop language skills. Students must know that their ideas are important and that their questions will be heard. Have fun and accept all reasonable answers while praising and encouraging questioning from the students.

Vocabulary Expansion

Describe and define these words and phrases:

relocate	CPR	good deed
army brat	911	misplace
narrate	emergency	accuse
impolite	despise	swipe
make miserable	accepted	horseplay

Language Expansion Activities

1. Get some clay and sculpt a horse that you think looks like Lady. Write a story about your horse.

2. Act out the story of Molly Manchester. Take turns playing the part of Molly. Tell how it feels not to be accepted by people you'd like to have as friends.

Language Expansion Questions

1. Who is telling the story? Who is listening to the story?

2. Why didn't the girls accept Molly at first?

3. Why did Molly always have to move? Does moving a lot sound exciting or scary to you? Why?

4. Molly performed CPR on Tam. Why is CPR something only someone who has had training should attempt? Would you like to be trained if/when you are old enough? Why or why not?

5. Molly tried to make friends with the girls, but they didn't accept her at first. Why? Has this ever happened to you? What did you do about it?

6. When Molly got home from school, she talked with her mom about her feelings. Do you have someone at home that you can talk to? Who is it? What do you talk about?

7. Molly had a pony. Many kids dream of owning a pony. What would you do if you could have your own pony?

8. Tam and her friends took her mom's ruby ring as a prank, but the story doesn't tell what the prank was. Make up a prank that might fit in the story. Explain why pranks aren't smart.

9. The girls had lost the ruby ring. They were scared. Have you ever lost something that wasn't yours? What should you do if you break or lose something that belongs to someone else?

10. At the end of the story, Pat told Trish to remember the story of Molly Manchester whenever Suzy wants to play with her. What lesson was Pat trying to teach Trish?

A STUDY BUDDY

UNIT 23

Phonology/Orthography Concepts

- When **-y** occurs at the **end** of a word, it represents a long vowel sound.
- At the end of a one-syllable word, **-y** represents long /i/.
- At the end of a word with more than one syllable, **-y** represents long /e/.

Vocabulary

army	Molly	sorry	*pretty*
buddy	my	story	*there*
by	myself	study	*Tuesday*
candy	nasty	Suzy	*Wednesday*
cry	play	try	*where*
curly	plenty	ugly	
dry	pony	way	
funny	ruby	worry	
Lady	say		
lucky	simply		

A STUDY BUDDY

Story Summary:

When he sees his friend Nick struggling in school, Al offers to help him. Nick has always had problems with reading, writing, and spelling. Nick's friend, Al, seems to learn more easily than Nick does. Al offers to become Nick's study buddy, but Nick is sure that he can't learn, and he doesn't like being embarrassed in front of his friends. Al wants to try to help, and he won't give up on Nick.

"I just cannot do this," Nick said to himself.

He got up from his desk at school. He felt angry. He was not thinking of the test, but of playing his sax.

Al and Nick were best pals. They were playmates before they entered school, and Al had sat by Nick in every class. Al could tell that Nick was very upset.

Al felt sorry for Nick. But they were taking a hard test and could not say anything. Ms. Silver's buzzer rang. Tuesday's spelling pretest was over. They would get it

back on Wednesday.

Nick felt bad. "It was pretty hard," he said as he gave his test paper to Ms. Silver.

Al grabbed Nick's arm when they got to their lockers.

"What's the matter, Nick?" said Al. "You did not finish your test."

"I just cannot spell!" said Nick, upset. "Letters get stuck in my skull and I cannot remember words like you can."

Al did not say anything. He would like to try to help Nick.

"I try, I absolutely try," said Nick. "But spelling and words are hard for me."

"Maybe I can help you," Al said. "I could be your study buddy."

Nick felt there was no way Al could help. "Thanks, but no thanks," Nick muttered. "I have to study by myself."

Al would not give up. "Well, Nick, I have some tricks to help with studying. Let me help. I would like to help you."

"Where could we go?" Nick asked.

"Well, it's Tuesday. I'll be home by 4 PM. Let's get together then," said Al. "We can work on spelling together. Come on over after school and we can study."

When he got home, Al yelled, "Where are you, Mom? Nick is coming over to study!" She was in the den. "What do you have for a snack?" he asked his mom.

A long time later, Al was upset. The milk on the table was not even chilly any more. Al had finished his snack. Where could Nick be? He had not come to study. His glass of milk just sat and sat.

Al's mom came into the den. His mom asked, "Where is Nick?"

"I don't understand where he could be," Al said. "I think there is a problem. What do you think?"

"Well, where do you think he is?" Al's mom asked him.

"Sometimes Nick plays his sax in his backyard when there is a problem."

"Go over there and get Nick. He may just lack the will to get started," she said.

On his bike, Al passed yard after yard yelling for Nick, but Nick was not there. Al parked his bike at Nick's and rang the bell. Nobody came, but Al could hear Nick's sax from the back. He ran to the backyard. Nick was there, playing his sax.

"Where were you?" Al asked.

 Nick did not say anything.

"I can help you," said Al. "I came this far. Will you just try with me?"

"Al, it is no use. I can play the sax. I can fix things. But forget spelling and tests. I'm not smart like you," said Nick.

"If you were not smart, you could not play the sax or fix things." Al turned and walked away.

Nick jumped up. He ran after Al. "You are super, Al," said Nick. "But I am just scared I will mess up and not pass."

Al gazed at him. "I do swell in math, but I cannot fix things like you can. You are fantastic at playing the sax and at fixing cars, but not so hot at spelling. So what? I think you should stick with it even when it gets hard. And you may even get better. I even fixed a lamp last summer."

Nick grinned. "Al, you never fixed any lamp." They both smiled.

"Well," said Al. "I did take a lamp apart. There were some pretty big problems getting it back together. You could have fixed it."

"OK, OK," said Nick. "I get your drift. I will study with you. I will try. But it will be hard. Don't get mad at me."

They rode bikes back to Al's.

As they sat at the desk in the den, Al got his spelling list from his backpack. "First, you give me the test, Nick," Al said. "Then, I'll give you one. That way we can memorize the words better. Deal?"

Nick smiled. It felt swell to have a study buddy's help.

Teacher/Parent Pages

Use the following questions to stimulate language growth, imagination, conceptual relationships, and higher-level thinking skills. These activities will encourage conversation and help develop language skills. Students must know that their ideas are important and that their questions will be heard. Have fun and accept all reasonable answers while praising and encouraging questioning from the students.

Vocabulary Expansion

Describe and define these words and phrases:

struggle	embarrassed	confront
stood up	ponder	flustered
lost in your thoughts	persistent	diversion
assignments	absolutely	persevere
stuck in your skull	strategy	commiserate

Language Expansion Activities

1. Write down all of the subjects you take in school. Then arrange them on a list, beginning with the easiest down through the hardest. Then, write: a) a paragraph explaining the things that seem most difficult about your hardest subject; or b) a paragraph explaining why your easiest subject might be hard for another person.

2. Draw a map of Nick and Al's neighborhood. Show the route Al had to go on his bicycle to get to Nick's house. Make up names of streets. Don't forget to put in parks, schools, and churches. Explain your map to everyone in your reading group.

Language Expansion Questions

1. What were Al and Nick doing at the beginning of the story? How do you know?

2. Nick was not thinking about his test. He was lost in his thoughts. What was he thinking about? Do you ever get lost in your thoughts? Write a story about the last time that happened.

3. Tests and quizzes are very hard for Nick, but he can play the sax well. Why do you think that's so? What is something you can do well? What is something that makes you struggle?

4. Why did Al want to help Nick?

5. Nick said, "Letters get stuck in my skull and I cannot remember words..." What did he mean? Does that ever happen to you? Explain what happens.

6. At first, Nick did not want Al to help him. Why do you think he turned down Al's offer to help him?

7. Read the third page of the story. How can you tell that Nick had stood Al up? Has anyone ever stood you up? How did you feel?

8. Al was persistent. He would not give up. In the end, he really helped Nick with his spelling. Why is it good to be persistent? When might it be smarter not to be so persistent?

9. Al confronted Nick with the fact that he had stood him up. It is not easy to confront someone. Have you ever confronted someone about something they had done to you? Tell about it.

10. Tell how you might have helped Nick with his spelling. How do you study for spelling tests?

A TRAIN TRIP

UNIT 24

Phonology/Orthography/Syllable Concepts

- Review: consonant digraphs: two consonant letters that represent one sound
- Vowel digraphs: two vowel letters that represent one long vowel phoneme
- A syllable that contains a vowel digraph (vowel team) is a **vowel digraph syllable**.

Vocabulary

barley	delay	lie	real	steak	*almost*
Bea	die	lower	rear	steam	*although*
beat	drain	may	relay	Sunday	*always*
beef	each	near	remain	tea	*does*
belief	elbow	own	repeat	three	*whom*
blow	feel	pain	road	throw	
board	feet	parsley	roast	tie	
boat	fellow	peace	say	today	
braid	field	peach	scream	toe	
brain	float	peanut	screen	tomatoes	
break	grain	peas	sea	train	
brief	great	pie	seat	turkey	
buy	green	please	see	wait	
chair	greet	potatoes	seem	waited	
cheer	guy	queen	seen	waiter	
clean	heel	rail	sheet	way	
clear	hoe	railing	shriek	wheat	
coach	key	rain	soak	year	
coat	lay	raise	Spain	yellow	
coffee	leave	reach	speak		
day	levee	read	stay		

A TRAIN TRIP

Story Summary:

Chick Miller, his wife, Pam, and his son, Mat, take a train trip to Ohio to attend Pam's mom's sixtieth birthday party. Although there is a delay along the way, Pam, Chick, and Mat discover how wonderful it is to have each other for support.

Chick and Mat were still in the line for the train. They had waited a long time to get to the ticket window. "Three tickets for the Ohio Valley Express," Chick said.

"Will it be first class or coach, Mr. Miller?" asked the fellow at the window.

"First class, please. We are going to Mrs. Miller's mom's birthday party. She will be sixty on Sunday," Chick said.

Pam was waiting at the railroad car for Chick and Mat. Although it was a misty, gray day, Pam felt elated. She had not seen her mom or dad since her wedding.

"I wonder where Chick and Mat could be," Pam said to herself. She cared for Mat as if he were her own. It was as if Pam had become Mat's real mom.

Pam spotted them. They were soaked. "What was the big delay?" she asked them.

After they got on board, a waiter came to take orders for dinner. "What will it be?" he asked. "Roast beef or turkey? Green peas or parsley potatoes? Coffee or tea? We have homemade peach pie today."

Mat had never ridden on a train before. Chick and Pam had planned this trip by train so that Mat could see the seacoast and the wheat and corn fields of the Midwest.

"Say, Dad, this cabin is sort of like home. But where are the beds?" asked Mat, putting on his coat and tie for dinner.

Chick said, "We have three berths. They can be raised during the day, and when we go to sleep, we can lower them."

"Can I sleep in the lower berth, Dad?" Mat asked. "Are you two dressed for dinner yet? I am starving."

Chick grinned at Pam. "You are always starving," they said together to Mat.

Later, as they waited to be seated in the dining car, Pam and Chick were greeted by the waiter. "Does your boy get sick on a bumpy trip?" he asked them. "This storm could blow pretty mean."

The rain beat hard on the windows in the  dining car. Strong winds rocked the car. Pam tripped and almost broke her heel, but Chick got her by the elbow. "I had hoped we could see the seacoast," Chick said.

Just as they were seated, the train became dark. A baby began to scream.

Dishes and napkins were whirling and flying madly in the dining car.

"Just remain in your seats and stay calm." The speaker on the intercom was firm. "I repeat. Remain in your seats."

Pam held fast to Chick and Mat.

The train came to a sudden stop. Each waiter began to help clean up the mess. Lamps became dim, but they could see.

Back in the cabin, Pam asked Chick, "Does anybody think we will have a long delay? Whom could we ask? Do you think we will make it in time for my mom's birthday party on Sunday? When do you think we will get to Ohio, Chick?"

Mat felt restless. "If you read for a while, you'll get to sleep, Mat," Chick said, as he opened the lower berth.

When Mat and Pam woke up, Chick was not there. He went to check on the delay. "The train has not stirred," he said.

"Did you overhear what the guy was saying? The train was derailed by a mud slide. More than fifty men are working on the rails. They are almost finished. Does anybody want anything? I could always buy it in there and bring us a tray in here."

"Just coffee and raisin toast for me," Pam said.

Mat shot up. "I'm hungry! I think I want some oatmeal. Can I have toast and cocoa, too?"

When Chick left the car, Mat said, "Don't cry, Pam. I think we'll get to Ohio in time for

the birthday party.
Besides, they will not start
the party until we get
there!"

"Mat, you and Chick
are the best things that
have ever happened to me. You have made
me understand that being a mom can be
wonderful. Can I have a big hug?"

"You bet, Mom!" Before that moment, she
had always been Pam to Mat.

When the three of them stepped off the
train at the Ohio Valley platform, Mr. and
Mrs. Kipling and Pam's sister, Faith, were
there to greet them with lots of
hugs and kisses.

"Well, you three made it
just in time! Just wait until
you see what plans we have
in store for you."

Teacher/Parent Pages

Use the following questions to stimulate language growth, imagination, conceptual relationships, and higher-level thinking skills. These activities will encourage conversation and help develop language skills. Students must know that their ideas are important and that their questions will be heard. Have fun and accept all reasonable answers while praising and encouraging questioning from the students.

Vocabulary Expansion

Describe and define these words and phrases:

express train	coach	delay
felt elated	railroad car	felt restless
stepmother	waiter	overhear
mother-in-law	cabin	celebrate
first class	berth	

Language Expansion Activities

1. Ask the librarian to help you gather some information about trains. Make an oral report to the others in your class or group, and describe the differences between the first trains and modern trains.

2. At the top of a chart, print the different types of traveling (train, plane, etc.). Under each different type, list advantages and disadvantages of each type of travel. Explain how the distance you are traveling helps you decide what kind of travel is best for a trip.

Language Expansion Questions

1. What was the Ohio Valley Express? Based on the story, describe every detail you can remember about it.

2. Discuss the reasons why Pam, Chick, and Mat were going to Ohio. Recall your last trip and tell why your family went there.

3. Pam was Mat's stepmother. What does that mean? Do you know anybody who has a stepparent or stepsister or stepbrother? Think of some of the reasons why it might be hard to learn to live with somebody new in a family. What are some of the things that people can do to help them learn to live together happily?

4. How did the weather affect the Millers' train trip?

5. In the dining car, the menu gave the Millers several choices for dinner. If you had been with them, what choice would you have made? Plan your favorite menu and share with your friends the things you would include for your best meal ever.

6. During the storm, there was a speaker on an intercom that gave them instructions. Why are intercoms helpful in many situations?

7. Why was Pam so concerned about the delay? What event was everyone anticipating? Has such a delay ever happened to you?

8. Mat told Pam, ". . . they won't start the party until we get there!" What did he mean by that? Would the others really wait for them?

9. Weather can cause many kinds of disasters. Discuss some of the weather-related disasters that you've heard about on the news.

10. At the end of the story, Mat says to Pam, "You bet, Mom!" Explain why what Mat said to Pam was so important. How do you think it made Pam feel?

Unit 24, Book 2

ON BOARD THE RIVER QUEEN

UNIT 24

Phonology/Orthography/Syllable Concepts

- Review: consonant digraphs: two consonant letters that represent one sound
- Vowel digraphs: two vowel letters that represent one long vowel phoneme
- A syllable that contains a vowel digraph (vowel team) is a **vowel digraph syllable**.

Vocabulary

barley	delay	lie	real	steak	*almost*
Bea	die	lower	rear	steam	*although*
beat	drain	may	relay	Sunday	*always*
beef	each	near	remain	tea	*does*
belief	elbow	own	repeat	three	*whom*
blow	feel	pain	road	throw	
board	feet	parsley	roast	tie	
boat	fellow	peace	say	today	
braid	field	peach	scream	toe	
brain	float	peanut	screen	tomatoes	
break	grain	peas	sea	train	
brief	great	pie	seat	turkey	
buy	green	please	see	wait	
chair	greet	potatoes	seem	waited	
cheer	guy	queen	seen	waiter	
clean	heel	rail	sheet	way	
clear	hoe	railing	shriek	wheat	
coach	key	rain	soak	year	
coat	lay	raise	Spain	yellow	
coffee	leave	reach	speak		
day	levee	read	stay		

134

ON BOARD THE RIVER QUEEN

Story Summary:

While Chick, Pam, and Mat Miller are on a trip to Ohio to visit Pam's parents, Bea and Leo Kipling, Mat takes a trip on the River Queen with his granddad and they have a big surprise along the way.

 Mr. Kipling, Pam's father, had promised Mat a trip on the River Queen, an Ohio River steamboat. Each Monday morning, it departed at ten o'clock sharp.

When they reached the dock, Granddad began telling Mat some Ohio River tales. "After this trip today, I hope you will feel as I do each time I take a ride on the river."

It was a clear, sunny day, and over the levee, they could see for miles. There were grain elevators, chimneys, and miles and miles of fields. "See the corn, beans, peas, oats, barley, and wheat, Mat," said Granddad, "These crops made the Ohio River Valley what it is today."

They boarded the River Queen at ten 'til ten, and the steamer began to shriek. Mat jumped up and nearly fell overboard! "Does that blast mean it's time to go?" he asked. Granddad grabbed Mat's elbow.

"You break me up, Mat!" said Granddad with a big grin. "The man at the helm always blows that horn just before he takes off, Mat. It's his warning to any ships on the River that the River Queen is leaving port."

"Is it almost time to eat the lunch that Grandmom packed us?" asked Mat. "I'm starved. I think she made me a peanut butter and jelly sandwich and packed me some potato chips and a peach."

"We just got on board, Mat! We just ate!" Granddad laughed. "But if you want to, have your sandwich. We can always go up to the top deck and get something more to eat later."

 The day was crisp. Wispy, white puffs swept by over them. Mat felt pure peace. Granddad was speaking to a man at the helm. Near the railing, Mat felt a soft spray from the river.

A gray-haired lady with a yellow throw over her feet lay back in her armchair on the deck. A tear dropped to her cheek. She seemed very sad. Mat could not understand why anyone could be unhappy on such a fantastic day as this.

"What's the matter, Ma'am? Can I help you? Can I get you something? Are you sick?" She seemed so unhappy, Mat decided to try to cheer her up.

"I'm Mat Miller, and I am visiting my granddad and grandmom. Is this your first time on the River Queen?"

"No, dear, I was born and reared here in Ohio. I feel like I could stand at the  helm of the River Queen myself!

"I have been away from this part of the world for 25 years, yet it almost feels like I never left," said the lady.

"Gosh, where were you for so long?" Mat asked.

"For many years, I lived in the Near East. I had a great life and traveled the world," explained the lady.

Mat felt almost as if he had met this lady before. He liked her.

"Do you see those big grain flatboats on the river, Mat? They will carry grain from the Midwest to the Gulf of Mexico. From there, big ships will deliver it to ports like Spain or the Netherlands.

 "That grain could even go to the Near East, where I used to live and work. I think I have been feeling a bit lonely sitting here. Since I retired and returned to Ohio last week, I have had a hard time finding any of my former school chums," the lady went on. "I was just feeling sorry for myself," she added.

At that very moment, Granddad came up to them and said, "There you are, Mat! I began to think that you had fallen in!"

"Granddad, this is . . . gosh, I did not even ask you your name!" Mat stuttered.

"Land sakes, is that really you, Jean Marlow?" Granddad said with a start.

"Leo Kipling," said the lady, rising from her deck chair, "it has been too long!"

"Mat, this is an old chum of mine and your grandmom's, Jean Marlow. Jean had more brains than any other girl in our class . . . and more class, too, if I do say so myself. Just wait 'til we get back to the dock. What a surprise is in store for Grandmom. Bea will not believe this."

The three of them began to plan the surprise. "Leo, when we get to the dock, I'll hide behind you and Mat," Jean said. "Then, when Bea sees you, I'll rush up and give her a big hug!"

Teacher/Parent Pages

Use the following questions to stimulate language growth, imagination, conceptual relationships, and higher-level thinking skills. These activities will encourage conversation and help develop language skills. Students must know that their ideas are important and that their questions will be heard. Have fun and accept all reasonable answers while praising and encouraging questioning from the students.

Vocabulary Expansion

Describe and define these words and phrases:

steamboat trip	steamer	barges
Ohio River	felt pure peace	retired
depart	Near East	land sakes
the helm	traveled the world	old school chum
grain elevator	port	sternwheeler

Language Expansion Activities

1. At the library, find a map that shows the countries of the Near East. Have each person in your group make a report on one of the countries of the Near East. Tell about the people, the costumes, the customs, and the products of the country. Explain how the country is similar to and different from your own home.

2. Many kinds of boats and ships travel up and down big rivers and on the ocean. Find some pictures of different kinds of boats and ships. Make a booklet with your pictures, and discuss the different vessels with your group.

Language Expansion Questions

1. What was Mat's stepgrandfather's name? What did Mat call him? What are some other names that we call our grandparents?

2. What Ohio River Valley crops did Granddad tell Mat about? Explain what he meant when he said, "These crops made the Ohio River Valley what it is today."

3. "Mat felt pure peace." What did this mean? Have you felt it?

4. Explain why Mat decided to try to cheer up the unhappy lady sitting on the deck. Why was she unhappy?

5. On a map of the USA, find the Ohio River and the Gulf of Mexico. Trace the routes that the barges, or big grain flatboats, use to carry grain from Ohio for shipping to other countries.

6. What was the big surprise that Granddad and the lady had for Mat's grandmom? How did Jean Marlow know Mat's granddad and grandmom? Describe how those older people must have felt.

7. What is special about being reunited with an old friend? Has that ever happened to you? Try to remember how you felt.

8. There are many reasons why people might move away from their homes. Think of as many reasons as you can. Has anybody in your family ever moved away? Where did they move?

9. Do you think that Jean Marlow had an exciting life? What are the pros and cons of traveling around the world?

10. If you decided to become a riverboat pilot, what are some of the things you would have to learn? Make a list of them.